DANTE WOODSON

Keep Up

Breaking the Cycle of Financial Hardship

Copyright © 2024 by Dante Woodson

All rights reserved. No part of this publication may be reproduced, stored or transmitted in any form or by any means, electronic, mechanical, photocopying, recording, scanning, or otherwise without written permission from the publisher. It is illegal to copy this book, post it to a website, or distribute it by any other means without permission.

Dante Woodson asserts the moral right to be identified as the author of this work.

Dante Woodson has no responsibility for the persistence or accuracy of URLs for external or third-party Internet Websites referred to in this publication and does not guarantee that any content on such Websites is, or will remain, accurate or appropriate.

Designations used by companies to distinguish their products are often claimed as trademarks. All brand names and product names used in this book and on its cover are trade names, service marks, trademarks and registered trademarks of their respective owners. The publishers and the book are not associated with any product or vendor mentioned in this book. None of the companies referenced within the book have endorsed the book.

First edition

ISBN: 979-8-34-027052-8

*This book was professionally typeset on Reedsy.
Find out more at reedsy.com*

Contents

1	The Historical Context of Financial Hardships	1
2	The Psychology of Money: Breaking Mindset Barriers	7
3	Consumerism's Impact on Financial Freedom	13
4	Budgeting Isn't Boring	20
5	How to Escape Debt and Build Wealth	29
6	The Power of Ownership & What Generational Wealth Really...	36
7	Investing 101: Making Your Money Work for You	43
8	Side Hustles and Entrepreneurship: Building Multiple Income...	51
9	Planning for the Future: The Role of Estate Planning and...	59
10	Conclusion: Reclaiming Financial Power	67
Back Matter		72
Notes		74
Notes		75
Notes		76

1

The Historical Context of Financial Hardships

When we talk about the financial hardships faced by minority communities, we're not just talking about personal struggles with money. We're talking about a legacy of systemic barriers that have deliberately and consistently made it harder for Black and Brown families to build and retain wealth. These barriers didn't just appear overnight; they were woven into the fabric of American society over generations, creating a lasting impact that continues to shape the financial landscape for minority communities today.

To understand why financial freedom feels so out of reach for many of us, we need to start by looking at the past. The structural forces that held our communities back aren't abstract concepts—they are real, tangible policies and practices, like redlining, wage disparities, and lack of access to credit, that have left a ripple effect we still feel today. Understanding these forces is critical to moving forward and reclaiming financial power.

Redlining: The Legacy of Exclusion

One of the most blatant examples of how systemic barriers were erected against minority communities is **redlining**. In the early 20th century, homeownership was promoted as a key pillar of the American Dream—a way to build wealth and pass it down to future generations. But for many Black families, that dream was made nearly impossible to attain.

Redlining was the practice of denying loans and financial services to people living in certain neighborhoods, which were often predominantly Black and Latino. In the 1930s, the federal government created color-coded maps to help lenders determine which areas were "high-risk" for mortgage lending. Neighborhoods that were predominantly white were coded in green, signaling them as safe investments. On the other hand, neighborhoods where Black and Latino families lived were outlined in red, marking them as "hazardous" and effectively shutting them out from home loans, even if the families had good credit and savings.

For example, between the 1930s and the late 1960s, more than 98% of loans approved by the government-backed Home Owners' Loan Corporation went to white applicants. Black families, no matter how financially stable, were forced to rent or live in overcrowded neighborhoods with declining property values. This systemic denial of homeownership meant that Black families were locked out of one of the most common avenues of wealth-building in America: property appreciation.

The ripple effects of redlining are still felt today. A 2020 study found that formerly redlined neighborhoods are still more likely to be lower-income and have lower property values than their non-redlined counterparts. In cities like Chicago, Detroit, and Philadelphia, many Black families are still living in neighborhoods that were once redlined, limiting their opportunities for wealth accumulation and upward mobility.

Wage Disparities: The Value of Our Labor

Another key factor contributing to financial hardship in minority communities is **wage disparity**. Black and Latino workers have long been paid less than their white counterparts for doing the same jobs. Even today, these wage gaps persist. As of 2020, Black men earned about 87% of what white men earned, while Black women earned just 63% of what white men earned. Latino workers, particularly women, fared even worse.

This wage gap is not just about unequal pay for equal work. It also speaks to the kinds of jobs that minority workers have historically been relegated to. For decades, Black and Latino workers were concentrated in lower-paying, less stable jobs—jobs that didn't come with benefits like healthcare, retirement plans, or paid time off. These jobs also made it harder to accumulate savings or invest in wealth-building opportunities like homeownership or education.

Think about this: over a 40-year career, the typical Black worker stands to lose nearly $1 million in lifetime earnings due to wage disparities. That's $1 million that could have been used to buy a home, invest in the stock market, or pay for a child's college education. The cumulative effect of these wage disparities is a major contributor to the racial wealth gap we see today.

Lack of Access to Credit

Even when minority communities manage to save or stabilize their income, another barrier emerges: **lack of access to credit**. Historically, banks and lending institutions have been reluctant to offer loans, lines of credit, or favorable terms to minority borrowers. This systemic exclusion has been a major roadblock for families trying to build wealth through business ownership, education, or property investment.

Even when minority families do gain access to credit, they are often subject to predatory lending practices. High-interest loans, payday lending, and balloon payment mortgages disproportionately target Black and Latino borrowers, trapping them in cycles of debt. In 2017, for example, Black homebuyers were more than twice as likely to be denied a conventional mortgage as white homebuyers, even when controlling for income and credit scores. Those who were approved often faced higher interest rates, meaning they paid more over the life of the loan for the same home.

The lack of access to fair credit options also extends to businesses. Minority entrepreneurs often find it harder to secure loans to start or grow their businesses. This prevents many from taking the leap into entrepreneurship, one of the key pathways to building generational wealth. When they are able to secure loans, the terms are often less favorable, with higher interest rates and stricter repayment schedules, which hampers their ability to expand and scale.

The Ripple Effect: Today's Financial Landscape

These barriers didn't just affect past generations—they continue to shape the financial realities of minority communities today. **The racial wealth gap** is stark: the median wealth of a white family in the U.S. is 10 times greater than that of a Black family and 8 times greater than that of a Latino family. This isn't just the result of individual financial decisions; it's the cumulative effect of centuries of systemic exclusion from wealth-building opportunities.

Consider this: by the time the Fair Housing Act was passed in 1968, white families had already been benefiting from decades of homeownership and property appreciation, giving them a significant head start in wealth accumulation. Meanwhile, Black families who had been denied those opportunities were left playing catch-up. And while policies like the Fair Housing Act and the Equal Credit Opportunity Act were supposed to level the playing field, their impact has been limited by ongoing discriminatory practices in lending, real estate, and employment.

The result? Minority communities remain disproportionately burdened by poverty, housing instability, and financial insecurity. Without access to the same wealth-building tools—like homeownership, fair wages, and credit—these communities are left struggling to build the kind of financial stability that is taken for granted by others.

Moving Forward: Understanding the Barriers to Reclaim Power

Understanding the historical context of these financial hardships is crucial to reclaiming financial power. The barriers that have been placed in front of minority communities are real, but they are not insurmountable. The key to overcoming them lies in recognizing their impact and taking intentional steps to build wealth for ourselves and future generations.

By knowing where we came from, we can better understand where we need to go. It starts with reclaiming control over our financial decisions—whether that's budgeting more effectively, investing in homeownership, or seeking fair credit opportunities. The road to financial freedom may be steep, but it is one we can navigate by learning from the past and committing to a future of empowerment and wealth-building.

2

The Psychology of Money: Breaking Mindset Barriers

Money is more than just numbers in a bank account. It's deeply emotional, tied to how we see ourselves, our status, and our place in society. For many of us, our relationship with money is shaped by our upbringing and environment. Whether we grew up in households where money was scarce or abundant, the habits and beliefs we learned in those formative years can follow us throughout our lives. These beliefs influence how we save, spend, and think about wealth.

The tricky part is that most of us are unaware of how deeply these money scripts—mental narratives about money—affect our financial decisions. For minority communities, this relationship with money is often complicated by generational trauma, systemic barriers, and the societal pressure to "keep up." Breaking free from these mindset barriers is the key to building financial freedom.

The Scarcity Mindset vs. The Abundance Mindset

At the heart of our relationship with money is something called the **scarcity mindset**. This is the belief that there's never enough—that resources like money are finite and hard to come by. When you're stuck in a scarcity mindset, every dollar spent feels like a loss, and every financial decision is made with fear. This mindset is common among people who grew up in environments where money was tight, where financial instability was a constant presence.

When you've been taught that money is always running out, it's easy to fall into survival mode, focusing only on getting by in the short term. This often leads to behaviors like **emotional spending**—using money as a way to cope with stress or as a temporary escape from financial worries. For example, buying something new, like clothes or gadgets, can give us a quick boost of happiness, a feeling of control when everything else seems out of reach. But that joy is fleeting, and we're often left with regret and a dwindling bank account.

The scarcity mindset also affects how we approach opportunities. When you're constantly worried about not having enough, it's hard to take risks—like starting a business, investing, or pursuing a new career. Instead, we stick to what feels safe, even if it's not serving our long-term financial goals.

Contrast this with the **abundance mindset**, which is rooted in the belief that there are enough resources to go around. People with an abundance mindset see opportunities where others see limitations. They are more likely to invest in themselves, take calculated risks, and see setbacks as learning experiences rather than roadblocks. This mindset isn't about pretending that money isn't an issue; it's about believing that with the right tools and effort, financial stability is achievable.

For many of us, shifting from scarcity to abundance is a necessary first step to reclaiming our financial power.

The Role of Upbringing and Environment

Our childhood experiences around money play a huge role in shaping our financial mindset. If you grew up in a household where money was always tight, you may have internalized a sense of fear or shame around money. Hearing phrases like "money doesn't grow on trees" or "we can't afford that" on repeat can embed the idea that financial success is out of reach.

In contrast, those who grew up in environments where money was openly discussed and financial decisions were planned out tend to approach money with more confidence. They've seen the benefits of saving, investing, and living within their means, so they're more likely to follow those habits in adulthood.

But let's be clear—our upbringing isn't the final word on our financial future. While it can influence us, we have the power to unlearn those limiting beliefs and replace them with healthier, more productive habits.

Emotional Spending and Societal Pressure

Emotional spending is one of the most common manifestations of the scarcity mindset. When money is tight, we're often bombarded with a mix of anxiety, guilt, and the need to escape. Spending money can provide temporary relief from that anxiety—whether it's buying something small to feel in control or splurging on a bigger purchase to reward ourselves for hard work.

However, this kind of spending often leads to a cycle of guilt and regret. We feel guilty for spending money we don't have, which leads to more stress, which leads to more spending to cope with that stress. This vicious cycle is hard to break, especially when society pressures us to "keep up" with others.

Social media amplifies this pressure. It's easy to scroll through Instagram and see influencers flaunting luxury cars, designer clothes, and expensive vacations. Even if we know that much of what we see online is curated or exaggerated, the constant exposure can make us feel like we're falling behind if we're not able to afford the same things.

The truth is, **keeping up with the Joneses** (or the Kardashians, in today's world) is a losing game. The more we chase after material things to prove our worth, the further we move away from true financial freedom. The key is to recognize that real wealth isn't about what you can show off; it's about the security and freedom you build for yourself and your family.

Shifting the Mindset: Tools for Change

So, how do we break free from the scarcity mindset and start thinking with abundance? It starts with awareness—recognizing the thought patterns and habits that are holding you back. Once you become aware of these patterns, you can begin to replace them with more empowering beliefs and actions.

Here are a few tools to help shift your mindset:

1. **Identify Your Money Story**: Take a moment to reflect on your earliest memories of money. What did your parents or caregivers teach you about money, either directly or indirectly? How did those experiences shape the way you think about money today? Understanding your money story is the first step in rewriting it.
2. **Practice Gratitude**: Gratitude is a powerful tool for shifting from scarcity to abundance. When we focus on what we have rather than what we lack, it becomes easier to see opportunities rather than limitations. Each day, write down three things you're grateful for—whether it's a steady job, a supportive family, or the ability to save, even a little.
3. **Set Clear Financial Goals**: A key part of the abundance mindset is being proactive about your future. Instead of reacting to financial stress, create a plan. Set specific, measurable financial goals—like saving a certain amount by the end of the year or paying off a specific debt. Break those goals down into smaller, achievable steps.
4. **Separate Wants from Needs**: When you feel the urge to spend, ask yourself if the purchase is a want or a need. Will

this purchase bring you closer to your financial goals, or is it a temporary fix for an emotional need? This small act of reflection can make a big difference in your spending habits.
5. **Invest in Financial Education**: The more you know about how money works, the more empowered you'll feel. Read books, listen to podcasts, or take online courses on budgeting, investing, and wealth-building. The more educated you are, the easier it will be to shift from a scarcity mindset to an abundance mindset.

Breaking the Cycle

Breaking the mindset barriers that hold us back from financial freedom isn't easy, but it's essential. By understanding how our upbringing, environment, and emotions influence our relationship with money, we can start to take control of our financial future. The shift from scarcity to abundance is not about ignoring the challenges we face—it's about facing those challenges with the belief that we can overcome them.

With the right mindset, we can stop letting money control us and start using it as a tool to build a better future. Financial freedom begins with changing how we think about money, and that change starts today.

3

Consumerism's Impact on Financial Freedom

In today's world, we're constantly surrounded by messages telling us to buy more, do more, and have more. Consumerism—the relentless push to spend—is everywhere, from the billboards on the highway to the ads we scroll past on our phones. It tells us that happiness and success come from what we own, that we are defined by the brands we wear, the cars we drive, and the gadgets we use. For many people, this message is powerful, and it leads us into a cycle of spending that feels impossible to break.

In minority communities, the impact of consumerism is particularly significant. After generations of being denied access to wealth-building opportunities, there's an understandable desire to show the world that we've made it, that we're no longer struggling. But consumerism doesn't build wealth—it depletes it. The more we spend on things that don't appreciate in value, the harder it becomes to invest in ourselves and secure a better financial future.

The Role of Marketing and Social Media

The rise of marketing and social media has taken consumerism to a whole new level. Companies spend billions of dollars each year on targeted advertising designed to convince us that we need their products. Whether it's a flashy ad for the newest phone or a perfectly curated Instagram post showcasing luxury fashion, the message is always the same: "You'll be happier, more successful, more attractive—if you buy this."

Marketing taps into our emotions. It makes us feel like we're missing out, like we're behind everyone else if we don't have the latest and greatest. Social media amplifies this by putting everyone's best moments on display. We see our friends posting pictures of expensive vacations, new cars, and designer clothes, and it's easy to feel like we need to keep up. What we don't see are the credit card bills, the stress of living paycheck to paycheck, or the anxiety of not being able to save for the future.

This phenomenon, often called "keeping up with the Joneses," has been amplified by the digital age. The constant comparison to others—whether they're influencers or people in our social circles—drives many of us to spend money we don't have on things we don't need, all in an effort to maintain appearances. But the truth is, consumerism doesn't bring long-term happiness. It gives us a quick hit of satisfaction, but that feeling fades quickly, leaving us with buyer's remorse and financial stress.

Consumerism as Escapism

For many people, consumerism becomes a form of **escapism**. When life is hard, when we're dealing with financial stress, personal struggles, or societal pressures, buying something new can feel like a small victory. It gives us a sense of control, a fleeting feeling of success. But the relief that comes from spending is temporary, and the underlying problems remain.

In fact, emotional spending can make things worse. When we're stressed or unhappy, it's easy to rationalize purchases we don't need as a way to cope. We convince ourselves that we deserve to treat ourselves after a tough day or that buying something new will make us feel better. But in reality, this behavior can trap us in a cycle of debt and financial insecurity.

This cycle is particularly dangerous because it distracts us from the real issues at hand. Instead of addressing the root causes of our financial struggles—like budgeting, saving, and investing— we mask the problem with spending. The more we rely on consumerism as a form of escape, the harder it becomes to invest in the things that truly matter, like building wealth for the future.

The Real Cost of Consumerism

The cost of consumerism isn't just financial; it's also emotional and psychological. When we spend money on things that don't add value to our lives, we're left feeling unfulfilled. We might feel a brief sense of satisfaction when we buy a new gadget or outfit, but that feeling fades quickly, leaving us searching for the next purchase to fill the void. Over time, this can lead to a sense of emptiness and dissatisfaction with life.

Financially, the impact is even more damaging. Every dollar spent on things that don't appreciate in value is a dollar that could have been invested in something that does—like real estate, stocks, or even a savings account. Consumerism keeps us focused on the short-term, making it harder to plan for the future. It leads to a mindset where we prioritize immediate gratification over long-term financial security.

For many of us, the cost of consumerism also comes in the form of **debt**. Credit cards make it easy to spend money we don't have, and high-interest loans can quickly turn a small purchase into a financial burden. The average American carries over $6,000 in credit card debt, and minority communities are often hit even harder by predatory lending practices that make it difficult to escape the cycle of debt.

Let's not forget that consumerism is a never-ending game. Once we buy something, there's always something newer and better right around the corner. The pressure to keep up never stops. But the more we chase material things, the further we move from true financial freedom.

Investing in Yourself Instead of Stuff

Breaking free from consumerism requires a fundamental shift in mindset. Instead of focusing on what we can buy, we need to start focusing on what we can build. Every dollar we spend on material things is a missed opportunity to invest in something that will grow in value over time. The key to financial freedom isn't in buying more stuff—it's in investing in yourself and your future.

One of the best ways to break the cycle of consumerism is to start thinking about **opportunity costs**. For example, let's say you're tempted to buy the latest smartphone, which costs $1,000. Instead of making the purchase, consider what else you could do with that $1,000. You could invest it in a stock or mutual fund, where it has the potential to grow over time. You could use it to start an emergency savings fund or put it toward paying off debt. Each of these options will provide long-term benefits that far outweigh the temporary satisfaction of a new phone.

It's also important to start viewing money as a tool, not just something to be spent. Money can be used to create more opportunities—whether it's starting a business, investing in real estate, or taking a course to improve your skills. When you invest in yourself, you're not just spending money—you're building wealth and setting yourself up for long-term success.

Steps to Break Free from Consumerism

Breaking free from the consumerism trap isn't easy, especially when we're constantly bombarded with messages telling us to spend. But it's possible, and it starts with small, intentional changes in how we think about money.

1. **Practice Mindful Spending**: Before making a purchase, take a moment to ask yourself if it's something you really

need or if it's something you're buying out of emotion or societal pressure. If it's the latter, try delaying the purchase for a few days. More often than not, you'll find that the urge to buy fades.
2. **Focus on Long-Term Goals**: Keep your financial goals at the forefront of your mind. Whether it's saving for a house, starting a business, or investing for retirement, remind yourself that every dollar spent on unnecessary things is a dollar that could be helping you reach your goals faster.
3. **Limit Social Media Exposure**: Social media can be a major driver of consumerism. If you find yourself feeling envious or pressured to keep up with others, consider taking a break from platforms that encourage comparison. Focus on your own financial journey instead of what others are doing.
4. **Invest in Experiences, Not Things**: Research shows that people are generally happier when they spend money on experiences rather than material goods. Instead of buying things to impress others, focus on creating memories that will last. Travel, take up a hobby, or spend time with loved ones—these are the things that truly enrich our lives.
5. **Educate Yourself**: The more you know about how money works, the easier it becomes to resist the pull of consumerism. Educate yourself about personal finance, investing, and wealth-building. The more informed you are, the better equipped you'll be to make decisions that align with your long-term goals.

Breaking the Cycle

Consumerism keeps us trapped in a cycle of spending that ultimately robs us of financial freedom. The more we focus on buying things to impress others or escape our problems, the further we move from building real wealth. But by shifting our mindset, practicing mindful spending, and investing in ourselves, we can break free from this cycle and start creating a future of financial security and abundance.

True wealth isn't about what you own—it's about what you're building. It's time to stop chasing material things and start investing in the things that will truly make a difference in our lives and the lives of future generations.

4

Budgeting Isn't Boring

Let's be real: when most people hear the word "budgeting," their eyes glaze over. It sounds like a chore, something that takes the fun out of life, like a parental scolding telling you what you *can't* do with your own money. But the truth is, budgeting isn't boring—it's empowering. It's the tool that allows you to have control over your finances, instead of feeling like your paycheck disappears faster than you can earn it. When done right, budgeting doesn't restrict you; it gives you freedom. The freedom to live comfortably, plan for the future, and—yes—still enjoy the things you love.

But before we dive into the "how" of budgeting, let's talk about why so many of us think it's boring in the first place. Part of it comes from the fact that we've been sold this idea that spending is what makes life exciting. The shiny things, the big purchases, the instant gratification—we've been taught that's where the fun is. That's how we're supposed to measure success, right? The nice car, the expensive clothes, the nights out. But while these things might give us a quick dopamine hit, they don't provide lasting satisfaction.

For many minority communities, where generational wealth is rare and financial literacy isn't always a top priority, budgeting feels like a foreign concept. It's not something we were taught growing up. You learn how to survive—how to stretch a paycheck until the next one comes—but nobody talks about how to plan beyond that. A lot of us grew up in households where money was tight, where the conversation around finances was more about scarcity than abundance. So when we finally start making some money of our own, we want to enjoy it. And that's understandable. But enjoying your money doesn't mean blowing through it without a plan.

Take Angela, for example. Angela works a stable job, makes a decent income, but every month she finds herself wondering where her money went. Rent is paid, groceries are bought, and yet, by the third week of the month, she's already counting down the days until her next paycheck. She'll pick up the phone, open her banking app, and feel that sinking pit in her stomach when she sees how little is left. What happened?

Angela isn't careless with her money, but she's also not intentional. She doesn't have a budget. She's got a vague idea of her expenses and what she's spending, but it's more like playing a guessing game than following a plan. She's not alone. A lot of people operate this way, thinking they'll "just figure it out" as the month goes on. But that's where the trap is. Without a budget, you never truly know where your money is going. And more importantly, you don't know where it's *supposed* to go.

The thing is, budgeting isn't about restriction—it's about alignment. It's about making sure your money is working for you, instead of the other way around. When you don't budget, your money is in control. It's dictating what you can and can't do. But when you take the time to budget, you're the one in control. You tell your money where to go, and how much of it is going where.

Let's break this down. Imagine your financial life like a road trip. You've got a destination in mind—maybe it's buying a home, building up an emergency fund, or even just living comfortably without stressing about bills. If you don't have a budget, you're driving without a map. Sure, you might eventually get there, but it'll take longer, and you'll waste a lot of gas and time driving in circles. A budget is your roadmap. It shows you the most efficient way to get where you want to go, without getting lost along the way.

So, how do we start this process? How do we go from feeling lost in our finances to having a clear plan?

The first step is awareness. You have to know exactly where your money is going. This means tracking your spending—not just the big things like rent and bills, but everything. Every coffee, every takeout meal, every impulse Amazon purchase. It's easy to lose track of these small expenses, but they add up. And when you start seeing the numbers, you might be surprised at how much you're spending in areas you didn't even realize.

This is where the power of a budget comes in. Once you know where your money is going, you can decide if that's where you *want* it to go. Do you really want to spend $200 a month on takeout, or would you rather use that money to save for something more important? A budget allows you to make those choices consciously, rather than just reacting to what's left at the end of the month.

There are several popular budgeting methods, and the one you choose should depend on your personal financial situation and preferences. Below, we'll break down a few of the most common ones, with real-life examples to show how they can work for different income levels.

1. **The 50/30/20 Rule**

One of the simplest and most effective budgeting methods is the **50/30/20 rule**, popularized by Senator Elizabeth Warren. The idea is to divide your after-tax income into three categories:

- 50% for **needs**: This includes housing, utilities, groceries, transportation, and other essentials.
- 30% for **wants**: This covers non-essential spending like dining out, entertainment, and hobbies.
- 20% for **savings and debt repayment**: This portion goes toward building your savings, investing, or paying off debt.

Let's look at a real-life example for a **household** earning $50,000 a year (pre-tax), which translates to about $4,167 per month. Using the 50/30/20 rule, their budget would look something like this:

- $2,083 for needs (rent/mortgage, groceries, utilities, transportation)

- $1,250 for wants (dining out, streaming services, hobbies, vacations)
- $834 for savings or debt repayment (building an emergency fund, investing, or paying off credit cards)

This method is flexible, meaning that whether you're earning $2,000 or $4,000 a month, you can still apply these percentages to maintain a balance between needs, wants, and future financial security.

2. Zero-Based Budgeting

For those who want a more detailed and hands-on approach, **zero-based budgeting** might be the way to go. This method requires you to assign every dollar a job, so your income minus your expenses equals zero at the end of the month. Essentially, you're telling your money where to go, instead of wondering where it went.

Let's look at a **household** earning $4,000 a month. In a zero-based budget, every dollar is allocated to a specific category—whether it's rent, groceries, savings, or entertainment. Here's an example of how that might look:

- Rent/Mortgage: $1,200
- Groceries: $400
- Utilities: $200
- Transportation: $300
- Health insurance: $300
- Debt repayment: $500
- Savings: $400
- Entertainment: $300

- Miscellaneous: $400

At the end of the month, every dollar has a job, and nothing is left unaccounted for. Zero-based budgeting is especially effective for people who want to know exactly where their money is going, down to the last dollar.

No matter your income, zero-based budgeting ensures that every dollar is accounted for, giving you more control over your spending.

3. **The Envelope System**

If you prefer something more visual and tangible, the **envelope system** can be a helpful budgeting tool. This method involves physically dividing your money into envelopes for different spending categories. Once an envelope is empty, you can't spend any more in that category for the month.

Let's say a **household** has $4,000 in take-home pay for the month. Here's how the envelope system might work:

- Rent/Mortgage envelope: $1,200
- Groceries envelope: $500
- Utilities envelope: $200
- Transportation envelope: $300
- Savings envelope: $500
- Entertainment envelope: $300
- Miscellaneous envelope: $1,000 (for things like insurance, debt payments, and any other expenses)

In this system, once the grocery envelope is empty, no more

money can be spent on groceries until the next month. This method can be particularly effective for people who struggle with sticking to a budget and need a more hands-on way to manage their spending.

The envelope system works by making your spending more intentional, and it's a great way to curb impulse purchases.

Even with the best intentions, sticking to a budget can be hard. Unexpected expenses come up, old habits die hard, and it's easy to get discouraged when you don't see immediate results. But budgeting is a long game, and with some practice and patience, you can overcome these common challenges.

1. **Dealing with Irregular Income**: If your income fluctuates from month to month, it can feel impossible to stick to a budget. One way to handle this is by basing your budget on your lowest expected monthly income. If you earn more than expected one month, use the extra money to build an emergency fund or pay off debt.
2. **Handling Unexpected Expenses**: Life happens, and unexpected costs—like car repairs or medical bills—can throw a wrench in your budget. That's why it's crucial to build an emergency fund, even if you can only set aside a small amount each month. Having just $500 in an emergency fund can save you from going into debt the next time an unexpected expense pops up.
3. **Staying Consistent**: It's easy to stick to a budget for a month or two, but maintaining it long-term can be a challenge. The key is to review your budget regularly and make adjustments as needed. If you overspend in one

category one month, look for ways to cut back in another category next month. Flexibility is important, but so is accountability.
4. **Budget Burnout**: Budgeting fatigue is real. Sometimes, sticking to a budget feels restrictive, especially if it's tight. The key to avoiding burnout is to budget in some "fun money"—even if it's just a small amount. Having a little wiggle room for things you enjoy makes it easier to stay consistent in the long run.

One of the biggest misconceptions about budgeting is that it means giving up everything you enjoy. But that's not true at all. Budgeting isn't about depriving yourself; it's about being smart and intentional with your money. It's about making sure that your spending is aligned with your values and your goals. Maybe you love eating out, or maybe you're passionate about travel. A budget doesn't mean cutting those things out of your life—it means planning for them. It means making sure that when you do spend on the things you love, it's because you *can*, not because you're spending blindly and hoping it'll work out.

When you start budgeting, you begin to see the bigger picture. You start to realize that money is a tool, not a burden. It's something you can use to build the life you want, not something that controls you. And once you get into the habit of budgeting, it becomes second nature. You don't have to agonize over every purchase or obsess over every dollar. You just follow the plan, and the freedom that comes with that is far more satisfying than any impulse buy ever could be.

The truth is, budgeting isn't boring—it's the foundation for building financial freedom. It's what allows you to enjoy your money now, while also planning for the future. And once you see how much more control and peace of mind you get from budgeting, you'll wonder why you ever thought it was boring in the first place.

5

How to Escape Debt and Build Wealth

Debt has become a way of life for many people. Whether it's credit card balances, student loans, or high-interest payday loans, debt can feel like a never-ending cycle that keeps you from reaching your financial goals. For many, especially in minority communities, debt isn't just a burden—it's a trap. A system of predatory lending, rising education costs, and easy access to credit has made it difficult to escape this cycle, keeping people from building the kind of wealth that leads to financial freedom.

But here's the truth: while debt can be a heavy load, it doesn't have to be a life sentence. With the right strategies, it's possible to break free from debt and start building wealth at the same time. This chapter will dive into how debt affects wealth-building and provide clear, practical steps to help you eliminate debt and move toward financial security.

The Impact of Debt on Wealth-Building

Debt can be a major obstacle to wealth-building for several reasons. First, it eats into your income. Every dollar you send to a lender is a dollar that could have been saved or invested. When a significant portion of your monthly budget goes toward debt repayment, it's difficult to save for an emergency fund, invest in stocks, or even plan for retirement. Debt can keep you stuck in a paycheck-to-paycheck cycle, where every month feels like survival mode rather than a step toward financial freedom.

Second, debt can prevent you from taking financial risks that could lead to wealth. If you're overwhelmed by debt, you're less likely to invest in a new business venture or take out a mortgage to buy property. Even if these investments could pay off in the long run, the fear of adding more debt to your plate keeps you from making moves that could build wealth for the future.

Finally, debt—especially high-interest debt—makes it harder to reach long-term financial goals. Credit card debt, for example, often comes with interest rates of 15%, 20%, or even higher. At these rates, even a small balance can snowball into a significant financial burden. The more you pay in interest, the less you have to build wealth for yourself.

Common Types of Debt

Before we dive into strategies for getting out of debt, it's important to understand the types of debt that most people deal with and how they affect your financial situation:

1. **Credit Card Debt**: Credit cards are one of the most common sources of debt, and they're often the most expensive. With interest rates that can easily reach 20% or higher, carrying a balance on your credit card can quickly lead to overwhelming debt. The average American household carries about $6,000 in credit card debt, making it difficult to get ahead financially.
2. **Student Loans**: Student loans are often considered "good debt" because they allow you to invest in your education and future earning potential. However, with the rising cost of college tuition, student loan debt has reached crisis levels. Many people are burdened with tens of thousands of dollars in student loans, making it difficult to save, buy a home, or invest in other wealth-building opportunities.
3. **Predatory Lending**: Payday loans, auto title loans, and other predatory lending practices disproportionately target low-income and minority communities. These loans come with sky-high interest rates and fees, trapping borrowers in cycles of debt that are nearly impossible to escape. Even a small payday loan can balloon into a massive debt if it's not paid off quickly.
4. **Car Loans and Mortgages**: While car loans and mortgages are often seen as "necessary" debts, they can still hold you back from building wealth if not managed properly. Car loans depreciate in value as the car loses value over time, and overextending on a mortgage can leave you house-poor, with little left to save or invest.

Strategies to Break Free from Debt

Breaking free from debt requires a combination of practical strategies, discipline, and the right mindset. Here are some proven methods to help you tackle your debt and begin building wealth:

1. **The Debt Snowball Method**

The **debt snowball method** is a popular strategy for paying off debt, especially if you need quick wins to stay motivated. Here's how it works:

- List all of your debts, from smallest to largest, regardless of interest rate.
- Focus on paying off the smallest debt first while making minimum payments on the rest.
- Once the smallest debt is paid off, move on to the next smallest debt, applying the payments from the previous debt to the next one.

The idea behind the debt snowball method is that by quickly eliminating smaller debts, you build momentum and motivation. Seeing debts disappear one by one provides a psychological boost that can keep you focused and committed to your goal of becoming debt-free.

2. **The Debt Avalanche Method**

For those who are more focused on minimizing interest payments, the **debt avalanche method** may be a better choice. Here's how it works:

- List all of your debts in order of interest rate, from highest to lowest.
- Focus on paying off the debt with the highest interest rate first while making minimum payments on the rest.
- Once the highest-interest debt is paid off, move on to the next highest interest rate debt.

The debt avalanche method can save you money over time because it reduces the amount of interest you pay on your debts. While it may take longer to see a debt disappear (especially if the high-interest debt is large), this method is mathematically the most efficient way to pay off debt.

3. Consolidate or Refinance High-Interest Debt

If you're struggling with high-interest debt, such as credit card debt, consider **debt consolidation** or **refinancing** to lower your interest rates. Debt consolidation involves taking out a new loan to pay off multiple debts, combining them into one loan with a lower interest rate. This can simplify your payments and save you money on interest over time.

Refinancing works similarly but is often used for specific types of debt, like student loans or car loans. By refinancing, you may be able to secure a lower interest rate, reduce your monthly payments, or shorten the loan term, helping you pay off the debt more quickly.

4. Negotiate with Creditors

Many people don't realize that they can **negotiate with creditors** to reduce their debt. Credit card companies, in particular, are often willing to work with you if you're struggling to make payments. You may be able to negotiate a lower interest rate, a reduced balance, or a more manageable payment plan. It never hurts to call your creditor and ask for a break—they want to get paid, and they may be willing to work with you to make that happen.

5. **Increase Your Income**

While cutting expenses is important when paying off debt, don't forget the other side of the equation: **increasing your income**. This can be done through a side hustle, freelancing, or even asking for a raise at your current job. The extra income can be funneled directly into your debt repayment plan, helping you eliminate debt faster and freeing up more money to invest in your future.

6. **Build an Emergency Fund**

One of the biggest reasons people fall into debt is because of unexpected expenses—like medical bills, car repairs, or job loss. To prevent this from happening again, it's important to build an **emergency fund**. Even a small emergency fund of $500 to $1,000 can make a huge difference when life throws an unexpected expense your way. As you pay off debt, continue building this fund so that you have a financial cushion.

Building Wealth While Paying Off Debt

It may seem counterintuitive, but you don't have to wait until you're completely debt-free to start building wealth. In fact, it's important to **save and invest** while paying off debt, especially if you have low-interest debt like student loans or a mortgage.

Here's how you can do both:

1. **Save a Small Percentage of Your Income**: Even if you're focused on paying off debt, commit to saving a small percentage of your income—5%, 10%, or whatever you can manage. Over time, this money will add up, and you'll have a financial cushion for the future.
2. **Take Advantage of Employer Matches**: If your employer offers a 401(k) match, contribute enough to take full advantage of it, even while paying off debt. This is essentially free money, and it's a great way to start building your retirement savings.
3. **Invest in Low-Risk Options**: While aggressively paying down high-interest debt, consider investing in lower-risk, long-term assets like index funds or mutual funds. These investments grow over time and can help you start building wealth, even as you work to eliminate your debt.

Conclusion: Freedom from Debt, Path to Wealth

Debt doesn't have to define your financial future. By using strategies like the debt snowball or avalanche method, consolidating high-interest debt, and increasing your income, you can break free from the debt trap. Remember, it's not just about becoming debt-free—it's about building a foundation for long-term wealth at the same time. With a solid plan and disciplined approach, you can eliminate debt and start moving toward the financial freedom you deserve.

6

The Power of Ownership & What Generational Wealth Really Means

Ownership is the foundation of wealth. When we think about wealth, we often imagine luxury items like big houses, expensive cars, and lavish vacations. But real wealth isn't about these flashy displays—it's about owning assets that grow in value and provide financial security for the long term. For minority communities, especially those who have historically been excluded from ownership opportunities, understanding and harnessing the power of ownership is crucial in building and sustaining generational wealth.

Generational wealth is about more than just money in the bank. It's the accumulation of assets like property, stocks, businesses, and even intellectual property that can be passed down to future generations. By owning assets that appreciate over time, you not only build wealth for yourself, but you create a legacy that can provide for your children, grandchildren, and beyond. In this chapter, we'll explore the importance of ownership, discuss the different types of assets that build wealth, and explain the steps you can take to create generational wealth for your family.

What Does Ownership Mean?

Ownership goes beyond simply possessing material things. When you own an asset—whether it's a home, a piece of land, shares in a company, or a business—you have control over something that can grow in value. You're not just working for someone else's gain; you're building something that can benefit you and your family for years to come.

Let's take real estate as an example. If you're renting a home, every payment you make goes toward someone else's mortgage. You're essentially helping the landlord build their wealth. But when you own a home, each payment you make helps you build equity. Equity is the portion of the home that you truly own, and as property values rise, the value of your equity increases. This is one of the most straightforward ways that ownership builds wealth over time.

The same principle applies to owning shares in a company or running your own business. When you own shares, you have a stake in the company's growth, and as the company succeeds, so does the value of your investment. Owning a business allows you to generate income independently, and if the business is successful, it can provide a source of wealth that lasts for generations.

Types of Ownership That Build Wealth

There are several types of assets that contribute to building generational wealth. Let's dive into some of the most common ones:

1. Real Estate

Owning property is one of the most traditional and stable ways to build wealth. Real estate tends to appreciate in value over time, meaning that as years go by, the value of your property increases. This is especially true in areas that are developing or where housing demand is high. Real estate also offers immediate benefits, like the ability to rent out the property for additional income.

For many families, homeownership has been the first step toward building generational wealth. Consider a family that buys a home for $200,000. After 20 years, the home's value has increased to $400,000. The family now has $200,000 in equity, which they can use to sell the home, invest in another property, or pass down to their children. This is how generational wealth starts—by owning something that grows in value.

2. Stocks and Bonds

While real estate is a tangible asset, **stocks and bonds** allow you to participate in the financial markets and grow your wealth without managing physical property. Stocks represent ownership in a company, and as the company grows, so does the value of your shares. Bonds, on the other hand, are loans you give to companies or governments, which they repay with interest over time.

Investing in the stock market can be intimidating if you're not familiar with it, but it's one of the best ways to grow your wealth long-term. Many people start small, investing as little as $50 or $100 per month into index funds or mutual funds. Over time, these investments compound, growing your wealth faster than savings accounts alone can.

3. Small Businesses

Owning a business, even a small one, can be a powerful way to build wealth. When you run a business, you're not just generating income from your labor—you're creating an asset that can grow and generate wealth independently. A successful business can be passed down to your children, creating opportunities for future generations.

Think about how many small businesses are family-run. These businesses often start as a side hustle or small endeavor but grow into something that provides income for the entire family. Whether it's a restaurant, a cleaning service, or an online store, businesses have the potential to build wealth that lasts beyond one generation.

4. Intellectual Property

While real estate, stocks, and businesses are more traditional forms of ownership, **intellectual property** is another way to build wealth. Intellectual property includes creations of the mind—like inventions, designs, books, songs, or patents—that are legally protected and can generate income. Once you own intellectual property, you have control over how it's used, and you can earn royalties or licensing fees from others who want to use your creation.

For example, if you write a book or create a product that becomes popular, you can continue to earn money from that creation long after you've finished the initial work. Intellectual property can be passed down as part of your estate, providing income for your children and grandchildren.

Overcoming Barriers to Ownership

For many minority communities, achieving ownership hasn't always been easy. Systemic barriers like redlining, discriminatory lending practices, and lack of access to capital have historically kept Black and Brown families from owning property, starting businesses, or accumulating wealth.

For example, redlining was a practice where banks and lenders denied mortgages to people living in certain neighborhoods—often minority neighborhoods—effectively shutting them out of homeownership opportunities. Even today, the effects of redlining are still felt, as minority communities often have less access to loans and credit, making it harder to buy property or start a business.

But while these barriers are real, they're not insurmountable. Today, there are more resources available to help minority families break through these obstacles. First-time home buyer programs, grants for minority-owned businesses, and online investing platforms all offer opportunities to start owning assets, even with limited resources.

Steps to Building Generational Wealth

Building generational wealth starts with understanding how ownership works and taking small, intentional steps toward acquiring assets that grow in value. Here are some steps to get started:

1. **Start Small**: You don't need to buy a house or start a business right away. Start with what you have. If you can save a little each month, consider investing in low-cost index funds or putting money toward a down payment on a property.
2. **Educate Yourself**: Financial education is key to building wealth. Take the time to learn about how investments work, how to manage debt, and how to make your money grow. The more you know, the more confident you'll feel about making financial decisions.
3. **Plan for the Long Term**: Generational wealth isn't built overnight. It takes time, patience, and long-term planning. Whether you're investing in real estate, the stock market, or a business, think about the future and how these assets can benefit your family years from now.
4. **Protect Your Assets**: Building wealth is important, but so is protecting it. Make sure you have the right insurance, legal protections, and estate planning in place to ensure that the wealth you build can be passed down to future generations without unnecessary taxes or legal complications.

Conclusion: The Power of Ownership

Ownership is about more than just having something—it's about building a legacy. When you own assets that grow in value, you create opportunities for yourself and your family to achieve financial freedom. Whether it's real estate, stocks, a business, or intellectual property, ownership gives you control over your financial future. By taking small steps now, you can start building generational wealth that will benefit your family for generations to come.

7

Investing 101: Making Your Money Work for You

When people think about wealth, they often assume that it's something you have to work hard for—day in and day out, trading your time for money. But here's the secret that wealthy people understand: **your money can work for you**. Investing is one of the most powerful tools for building wealth, and it doesn't require a Wall Street-sized bank account to get started. Whether you're a seasoned investor or just starting out, understanding how to invest can make the difference between living paycheck to paycheck and building lasting financial security.

In this chapter, we'll break down the basics of investing, explain the different types of investments, and provide actionable steps to help you start making your money work for you. You don't need to be rich to invest—you just need the right mindset, a bit of patience, and a willingness to learn.

Why Investing Matters

Investing is the key to long-term wealth because it allows your money to grow over time. While saving money in a bank account is important, especially for emergencies, the interest you earn in a savings account is often too small to keep up with inflation. That means that the money you save today may lose value over time.

Investing, on the other hand, allows your money to grow faster than inflation. Through investments like stocks, bonds, and real estate, you can earn returns that increase the value of your money over time. The best part? The earlier you start, the more your money can grow thanks to **compound interest**.

Compound interest is like a snowball rolling downhill. When you invest, your money earns interest. That interest is then added to your original investment, and the next time, you earn interest on both the original amount and the interest. Over time, this compounding effect can turn a small investment into a substantial amount of money.

Types of Investments

There are several types of investments you can choose from, each with its own benefits and risks. The key is to understand how each investment works and to build a portfolio that suits your financial goals.

1. **Stocks**
   Stocks represent ownership in a company. When you buy a

stock, you're essentially buying a small piece of the company, and as the company grows and becomes more profitable, the value of your stock increases. Stocks tend to offer higher returns than other investments over the long term, but they can also be more volatile in the short term.

For example, let's say you buy 10 shares of a company at $50 per share. Over the next five years, the company's value increases, and the stock price rises to $100 per share. Your initial $500 investment is now worth $1,000, doubling your money without you having to lift a finger.

2. Bonds

Bonds are essentially loans you give to a company or government. When you buy a bond, you're lending money, and in return, the borrower agrees to pay you interest at regular intervals. Bonds are generally considered safer than stocks because they offer a fixed rate of return, but they tend to offer lower returns overall.

Bonds can be a good option for conservative investors who want a steady, reliable income without the risks associated with the stock market.

3. Mutual Funds and Index Funds

A **mutual fund** is a pool of money from multiple investors that's used to buy a diversified mix of stocks, bonds, or other securities. A professional fund manager decides which investments to make on behalf of the group. **Index funds** are a type of mutual fund that tracks a specific market index, like the S&P 500, which includes 500 of the largest companies in the U.S.

Both mutual funds and index funds are great options for beginner investors because they offer diversification, meaning your money is spread across many different investments. This reduces the risk of losing money if one investment performs poorly.

4. **Real Estate**

Real estate investing involves buying property, such as a home, apartment, or commercial building, with the goal of earning a return on your investment through rental income or property appreciation. Real estate is a tangible asset, meaning you can physically see and touch what you own, which makes it appealing to many people.

While real estate can provide steady income and long-term growth, it also requires more upfront capital and hands-on management compared to stocks or bonds.

5. **Retirement Accounts (401(k)s and IRAs)**

Retirement accounts, like a 401(k) or IRA, are tax-advantaged accounts that allow you to save and invest for retirement. A **401(k)** is typically offered by employers, and many companies offer matching contributions, meaning they'll add to your savings based on how much you contribute. An **IRA** (Individual Retirement Account) is similar but can be opened independently.

The key benefit of these accounts is that they offer tax advantages, meaning your money can grow tax-free or tax-deferred until you withdraw it in retirement.

How to Start Investing

Now that you understand the different types of investments, it's time to start putting your money to work. You don't need a lot of money to get started—thanks to technology, investing has never been more accessible. Here are a few simple steps to begin your investment journey.

1. **Start Small and Stay Consistent**
You don't need thousands of dollars to start investing. Many investment platforms allow you to start with as little as $10 or $20. The most important thing is to start early and stay consistent. The earlier you start, the more time your money has to grow.

For example, if you invest $100 per month starting at age 25 and earn an average annual return of 7%, you could have over $250,000 by the time you retire at age 65. Even if you don't have $100 to spare, investing a smaller amount each month can still grow into a significant sum over time.

2. **Take Advantage of Employer Retirement Plans**
If your employer offers a 401(k) plan, especially one with a matching contribution, take advantage of it. Employer matches are essentially free money, and they can significantly boost your retirement savings. Even if you can only contribute a small percentage of your income, it's worth it to start building your retirement fund.

3. **Use Low-Cost Investing Platforms**
Thanks to apps like Robinhood, Stash, and Acorns, it's easier

than ever to invest in the stock market without needing a financial advisor. These platforms offer commission-free trading, meaning you can buy and sell stocks without paying extra fees. Many of them also allow you to invest in fractional shares, meaning you can buy a portion of a stock even if you can't afford a full share.

Index funds and mutual funds are another great option for low-cost investing. Many index funds have very low fees, allowing more of your money to be invested rather than going toward management costs.

4. Diversify Your Portfolio

Diversification means spreading your investments across different types of assets to reduce risk. Instead of putting all your money into one stock or one type of investment, spread it out among stocks, bonds, real estate, and other assets. This way, if one investment performs poorly, the others can help balance out the loss.

Most financial experts recommend building a portfolio that includes a mix of stocks and bonds. Younger investors, with more time to recover from market downturns, may want to lean more heavily into stocks, while older investors may prefer a more conservative approach with a higher allocation to bonds.

5. Reinvest Your Earnings

When your investments generate dividends or interest, reinvest that money back into your portfolio. This allows you to take advantage of compound interest, which accelerates your wealth-building over time. Most investment platforms allow you to automatically reinvest dividends, so you don't even have to think about it.

Common Mistakes to Avoid

Investing can be intimidating, especially when markets fluctuate. Here are a few common mistakes to avoid:

- **Trying to Time the Market**: Many new investors try to buy stocks when prices are low and sell when they're high. But timing the market is extremely difficult, even for professionals. Instead, focus on long-term investing and stick to your plan, regardless of short-term market movements.
- **Overreacting to Market Swings**: It's normal for the stock market to go through ups and downs. Avoid the temptation to sell during a market downturn out of fear. Historically, the stock market has always recovered from downturns, and long-term investors who stay the course often see strong returns.
- **Putting All Your Eggs in One Basket**: Don't invest all your money in one stock or asset. Diversification is key to managing risk and protecting your investments.

Conclusion: Building Wealth Through Investing

Investing is one of the most powerful ways to build wealth, but it requires patience, discipline, and a long-term mindset. By starting small, staying consistent, and choosing investments that align with your goals, you can begin to make your money work for you.

Whether you're investing in stocks, real estate, or mutual funds, the earlier you start, the more time your money has to grow. Remember, the key to building wealth isn't about getting rich overnight—it's about making smart, consistent decisions over time.

8

Side Hustles and Entrepreneurship: Building Multiple Income Streams

For most of us, the idea of financial stability is tied to having a steady paycheck from a 9-to-5 job. But in today's world, relying on a single source of income can be risky. If anything were to happen to that job—whether it's layoffs, health issues, or an economic downturn—your entire financial stability could be jeopardized. This is why **multiple income streams** are a game-changer. Side hustles and entrepreneurship allow you to create additional sources of income, build wealth faster, and reduce your reliance on any one paycheck.

This chapter will explore the power of side hustles and entrepreneurship as tools for financial freedom. Whether you're looking to make a little extra cash on the side or build a full-blown business, diversifying your income is one of the most effective ways to reach your long-term financial goals.

Why You Need Multiple Income Streams

Having multiple income streams isn't just a strategy for the wealthy—it's essential for anyone who wants to build wealth and achieve financial security. A side hustle or entrepreneurial venture can provide an extra layer of protection if you lose your primary source of income, and it also offers the potential for significant financial growth.

There are several key reasons why building multiple income streams is crucial:

1. **Financial Stability**: Relying on a single paycheck makes you vulnerable to job loss or changes in the economy. Multiple income streams provide a safety net, allowing you to maintain financial stability even if one source of income dries up.
2. **Wealth Acceleration**: When you have more than one source of income, you can funnel extra money into paying off debt, saving, or investing. This accelerates your ability to build wealth and reach your financial goals faster.
3. **Opportunity for Growth**: Side hustles and businesses have the potential to grow into something bigger. What starts as a part-time gig could turn into a full-time business that generates substantial income, providing long-term financial security.
4. **Skill Development**: Running a side hustle or starting a business forces you to learn new skills, from marketing and sales to financial management. These skills not only make your business more successful, but they also increase your value in the job market, providing even more opportunities

for income.

What Is a Side Hustle?

A **side hustle** is any type of work or business you do outside of your primary job. Side hustles can range from freelance work to selling products online to offering services in your community. They're a flexible way to earn extra income while keeping your day job. The beauty of a side hustle is that it doesn't require a large upfront investment or a ton of time. You can start small, test the waters, and gradually scale it up as you gain experience.

Here are some examples of common side hustles:

- **Freelance Work**: If you have a skill like writing, graphic design, web development, or social media management, you can offer your services as a freelancer. Websites like Upwork and Fiverr make it easy to connect with clients looking for freelance help.
- **Ridesharing or Delivery**: Driving for rideshare services like Uber or Lyft or delivering food for apps like DoorDash or UberEats is a popular side hustle for people who want flexible hours and quick cash.
- **Online Stores**: Selling products online through platforms like Etsy, eBay, or Shopify is a great way to turn a hobby or skill into extra income. Whether it's handmade goods, vintage clothing, or digital products, online selling can be a lucrative side hustle.
- **Tutoring or Teaching**: If you're skilled in a particular subject, tutoring or teaching online can be a profitable side hustle. Platforms like VIPKid and Wyzant allow you to teach

students from around the world on your own schedule.
- **Service-Based Businesses**: Offering services like cleaning, lawn care, pet sitting, or home repairs in your local community can be a side hustle that provides steady, reliable income.

Starting a Side Hustle: How to Get Started

Starting a side hustle doesn't have to be complicated. Here's a simple step-by-step process to help you get started:

1. **Identify Your Skills and Interests**

The first step to starting a side hustle is identifying what you're good at and what you enjoy doing. Think about your skills, hobbies, and interests—these can often be turned into income-generating opportunities. For example, if you're great at photography, you could offer freelance photography services. If you love baking, you could sell baked goods to friends and family.

The key is to find something that you're passionate about and that has the potential to generate income. It's much easier to stay motivated when you enjoy what you're doing.

2. **Research the Market**

Once you've identified your potential side hustle, do some research to see if there's a demand for it. Who are your potential customers? What do they need? How much are they willing to pay? Researching the market will help you refine your idea and ensure there's a demand for your product or service.

For example, if you're considering starting a freelance graphic design business, research other graphic designers in your area or online. Look at their pricing, services, and customer reviews to get a sense of what clients are looking for.

3. **Start Small**

One of the biggest advantages of a side hustle is that you don't need to quit your day job or invest a lot of money upfront. Start small by offering your services to friends, family, or a few clients. Test your idea and refine it as you go.

Starting small also allows you to see if your side hustle is something you want to scale up. If it's successful, you can gradually invest more time and resources into it.

4. **Set Clear Goals**

Before diving into your side hustle, set clear financial and personal goals. Do you want to earn an extra $500 per month? Are you hoping to eventually turn your side hustle into a full-time business? Having clear goals will help you stay focused and motivated.

5. **Manage Your Time Wisely**

Balancing a side hustle with a full-time job can be challenging, so it's important to manage your time effectively. Set aside specific hours each week for your side hustle, and stick to that schedule. Time management tools like calendars, to-do lists, and productivity apps can help you stay organized.

From Side Hustle to Full-Time Business

While many people start side hustles to earn extra cash, others use them as a stepping stone to entrepreneurship. If your side hustle is successful, it can grow into a full-time business that provides a significant source of income. Here are some steps to take if you're ready to turn your side hustle into a full-time business:

1. **Scale Your Operations**

Once you've tested your side hustle and built a customer base, think about ways to scale your operations. This could mean increasing your production, hiring additional help, or expanding your marketing efforts. For example, if you run an online store, you could start selling on additional platforms or invest in digital advertising to reach more customers.

2. **Create a Business Plan**

If you're serious about turning your side hustle into a business, it's important to have a solid business plan. Your plan should outline your goals, target audience, marketing strategy, and financial projections. A business plan will also help you stay on track and secure funding if needed.

3. **Protect Yourself Legally**

When running a full-time business, it's crucial to protect yourself legally. This includes registering your business with the appropriate government agencies, obtaining any necessary licenses or permits, and setting up a separate business bank account. You may also want to consider business insurance to protect your assets.

4. **Reinvest Profits**

As your side hustle grows into a business, reinvest some of your profits back into the business. This could mean upgrading your equipment, hiring additional help, or investing in marketing to attract more customers. Reinvesting your profits will help your business grow faster and increase your income potential.

Overcoming Challenges in Entrepreneurship

Starting a business or running a side hustle isn't always easy. There will be challenges along the way, from finding customers to managing your time. But with persistence and the right strategies, these challenges can be overcome.

- **Finding Customers**: One of the biggest challenges for new entrepreneurs is finding customers. Start by leveraging your personal network—let friends, family, and coworkers know about your side hustle or business. You can also use social media, local advertising, and online platforms to reach a wider audience.
- **Time Management**: Juggling a side hustle with a full-time job can be exhausting. Set boundaries to ensure that you're not burning out. Prioritize tasks that will have the biggest impact on your business, and outsource smaller tasks if possible.
- **Dealing with Failure**: Not every side hustle or business idea will succeed right away, and that's okay. Failure is a part of entrepreneurship. Learn from your mistakes, adjust your approach, and keep moving forward.

Conclusion: Building Wealth with Multiple Income Streams

Side hustles and entrepreneurship offer incredible opportunities to build wealth, create financial security, and achieve independence. By diversifying your income streams, you're not just adding extra cash to your pocket—you're setting the foundation for long-term financial freedom. Whether you're starting small with a side hustle or going all-in on a business, the potential to grow your income and build wealth is in your hands.

9

Planning for the Future: The Role of Estate Planning and Insurance

When we talk about building wealth, most people think about making money—through investments, businesses, or real estate. But wealth-building doesn't stop there. It's not enough to accumulate assets; you need to protect those assets and ensure they are passed down to future generations. This is where **estate planning** and **insurance** come in.

Many people overlook these critical aspects of financial planning, thinking they're only necessary for the ultra-wealthy. But estate planning and insurance are essential for everyone, regardless of income level. These tools help ensure that the wealth you build during your lifetime is preserved and passed on, safeguarding your family's financial future. In this chapter, we'll dive into the basics of estate planning, wills, trusts, and life insurance, and explain how they can protect your family and your wealth.

What Is Estate Planning?

Estate planning is the process of preparing for the transfer of your assets after your death. It involves making decisions about how your money, property, and other assets will be distributed to your heirs and ensuring that your wishes are carried out. Estate planning can also involve setting up legal structures to minimize taxes, protect assets from creditors, and ensure a smooth transfer of wealth.

While it can be uncomfortable to think about, planning for the future is one of the most important steps you can take to protect your family. Without an estate plan, your assets could be tied up in probate for months—or even years—while your family struggles to cover expenses. Worse, your wealth could be divided in ways you didn't intend.

Here are some key components of estate planning:

Wills: The Foundation of Estate Planning

A **will** is a legal document that outlines how you want your assets to be distributed after your death. It's the most basic, yet essential, element of any estate plan. In your will, you can specify who will inherit your property, money, and personal items. You can also designate a guardian for your children, which is especially important if you have minor dependents.

Without a will, the court decides how to distribute your assets according to state law, which may not align with your wishes. This process is called **intestate succession**, and it can lead to unintended consequences, like estranged relatives receiving a portion of your estate or loved ones being left out altogether.

For example, if you pass away without a will and you're unmarried but have children, the court will determine how your assets are divided. If you're married, your spouse may receive everything, even if you wanted to leave part of your estate to other family members or causes you care about.

To create a will, you don't need to be wealthy or have a complex financial situation. In fact, it's even more important for individuals with modest estates to have a will to ensure that every asset, no matter how small, is distributed according to their wishes.

Trusts: Protecting Your Assets and Family

While a will outlines your wishes for distributing your assets, a **trust** is another estate planning tool that allows you to manage your assets during your lifetime and beyond. Trusts offer greater control over how and when your assets are distributed, and they can help minimize estate taxes and avoid probate, which is the court-supervised process of administering a will.

There are several types of trusts, but the two most common are **revocable trusts** and **irrevocable trusts**:

- **Revocable Trusts**: A revocable trust, also known as a living trust, allows you to maintain control over your assets during your lifetime. You can make changes to the trust, add or remove assets, and even dissolve it if necessary. After your death, the assets in the trust are distributed to your

beneficiaries according to the terms you've set. The main benefit of a revocable trust is that it helps your heirs avoid the lengthy and often expensive probate process.
- **Irrevocable Trusts**: Once you create an irrevocable trust, you can't make changes to it or access the assets within it. The primary advantage of this type of trust is that it can shield your assets from creditors and reduce estate taxes, making it a good option for those with significant wealth.

Trusts can also provide for specific situations, such as setting aside money for a child's education or ensuring that a spouse or dependent with special needs is taken care of after you're gone. For example, a **special needs trust** allows you to provide for a disabled loved one without jeopardizing their eligibility for government benefits like Medicaid.

Life Insurance: Securing Your Family's Future

Life insurance is a key component of any financial plan, especially for families who depend on your income. Life insurance provides a payout to your beneficiaries after your death, offering them financial support during a difficult time. This can be used to cover funeral expenses, pay off debts like a mortgage, or replace your income to help your family maintain their standard of living.

There are two main types of life insurance: **term life insurance** and **whole life insurance**.

- **Term Life Insurance**: Term life insurance provides coverage for a specific period, such as 10, 20, or 30 years. If you pass

away during the term, your beneficiaries receive the payout. Term life insurance is generally more affordable than whole life insurance and is a good option for families who need coverage during their prime earning years (for example, while raising children or paying off a mortgage).
- **Whole Life Insurance**: Whole life insurance, also known as permanent life insurance, provides coverage for your entire life. In addition to the death benefit, whole life policies include a savings component that grows over time. This savings feature allows you to build cash value, which you can borrow against or withdraw during your lifetime. While whole life insurance is more expensive than term insurance, it offers lifetime coverage and additional financial benefits.

For most people, term life insurance is sufficient and more affordable. The goal is to have enough coverage to ensure your family can cover essential expenses, such as housing, education, and daily living costs, in the event of your untimely death.

The Role of Beneficiary Designations

One often overlooked aspect of estate planning is ensuring that **beneficiary designations** are up to date on all your accounts. Beneficiary designations are commonly used for retirement accounts (like 401(k)s or IRAs), life insurance policies, and even certain bank accounts. These designations override what's written in your will, meaning that the assets in those accounts go directly to the named beneficiaries.

For example, if your 401(k) lists your ex-spouse as the beneficiary and you fail to update it after a divorce, they will still inherit the funds, regardless of what your will says. It's essential to review and update these designations regularly to ensure they align with your overall estate plan.

Minimizing Taxes and Legal Complications

Estate planning also involves minimizing the tax burden on your heirs. **Estate taxes** are levied on the transfer of your estate after death, and in some cases, they can significantly reduce the value of what you pass down. While federal estate taxes only apply to estates over a certain threshold (currently over $12 million in 2023), some states have lower thresholds for estate taxes.

Setting up trusts or gifting assets during your lifetime are ways to reduce the size of your taxable estate. For example, you can give up to a certain amount (currently $17,000 per recipient in 2023) to anyone you choose without paying gift taxes. Over time, these gifts can reduce the size of your estate, minimizing taxes and allowing you to pass more wealth to your family.

It's also important to work with an estate planning attorney to ensure that your estate plan is legally sound and meets all state and federal requirements. An attorney can help you navigate complex tax laws, avoid common mistakes, and ensure that your family is protected.

Protecting Your Wealth with Insurance

In addition to life insurance, other types of insurance are critical for protecting your wealth. **Disability insurance** can provide income if you're unable to work due to illness or injury, ensuring that you can continue to support your family and meet your financial obligations. **Homeowner's insurance** and **umbrella insurance** protect your property and assets from unforeseen events like accidents, lawsuits, or natural disasters.

Having the right insurance policies in place ensures that your wealth is protected, regardless of life's uncertainties. Without these safeguards, a single accident or illness could wipe out everything you've worked hard to build.

Estate Planning for Business Owners

If you own a business, estate planning becomes even more critical. A **succession plan** ensures that your business can continue to operate smoothly after your death. This plan may include naming a successor, outlining how ownership will be transferred, and ensuring that the business's assets are protected.

A trust can also help with business succession, allowing you to pass your business to your heirs without going through probate. This ensures that your business continues to thrive, providing income and stability for your family.

Conclusion: Planning for Tomorrow, Protecting Your Legacy

Building wealth is a significant achievement, but protecting that wealth and ensuring it's passed down to future generations is just as important. Estate planning and insurance are critical tools that allow you to safeguard your family's financial future and ensure that your legacy lives on. By creating a will, setting up trusts, securing life insurance, and working with professionals to minimize taxes, you can protect your assets and give your family the financial security they deserve.

Planning for the future isn't just about the wealth you accumulate—it's about the steps you take to ensure that wealth is protected and passed down to the people you care about most.

10

Conclusion: Reclaiming Financial Power

We've traveled a long road together, from understanding the historical roots of financial inequality to exploring the practical steps toward building wealth. If there's one thing you should take away from this book, it's that breaking the chains of consumerism and reclaiming financial power isn't an impossible dream. It's a journey—one that requires commitment, patience, and, most importantly, a mindset shift.

You've seen the data, the stories, and the steps laid out in front of you. Now, it's up to you to decide how to apply them. This isn't about becoming an expert in finance overnight or making a fortune tomorrow. It's about changing the way you think about money and wealth, recognizing the power of ownership, and committing to building something bigger than just a comfortable life today. It's about securing a future for yourself and the generations to come.

One of the biggest challenges for anyone on this journey is realizing that the financial narrative society has handed us isn't always designed for our success. In minority communities, the narrative often pushes us toward consumerism—encouraging us to spend money we don't have to prove our success or worth. But as you've learned, financial success doesn't come from outward displays of wealth. It comes from smart financial decisions, discipline, and owning assets that grow over time.

Taking control of your financial narrative starts with rejecting the idea that you need to "keep up" with anyone else. It's about creating your own path, based on your values and your goals. Whether it's building a business, investing in real estate, or simply sticking to a budget, your financial journey is your own. It doesn't matter where you start—what matters is that you start.

We've talked at length about the difference between being a consumer and being an investor, and this distinction is critical. It's easy to fall into the trap of spending because it provides a sense of immediate satisfaction. We're all guilty of it—whether it's buying that new gadget, upgrading our car, or splurging on a vacation. But the key to financial freedom is shifting from that consumer mindset to an investor's mindset.

Investors think long-term. They understand that the money they save today is money that can grow and provide for them tomorrow. They look for opportunities to put their money to work—whether through stocks, businesses, or real estate—and they know that ownership is the path to true wealth.

This shift in mindset is the foundation of everything we've discussed in this book. It's about recognizing that wealth isn't built through spending—it's built through investing in things that increase in value over time. If you can make this shift, you're already halfway to financial freedom.

Throughout this book, we've talked about generational wealth—what it is, why it matters, and how to achieve it. But it's important to remember that this isn't just about you. The financial decisions you make today have the power to affect your children, your grandchildren, and the generations that follow. By breaking the cycle of consumerism and focusing on ownership, you're not just changing your own life—you're changing the future of your family.

Imagine the impact of leaving your children a paid-off home instead of debt, or passing down an investment portfolio instead of a pile of unpaid bills. These are the things that create security and opportunity for future generations. They give your family the ability to focus on bigger dreams and goals, rather than struggling to get by. This is the legacy of financial freedom, and it's one you can start building today.

As we wrap up this journey, let's talk about what comes next. Reading this book is an important first step, but the real work begins with action. Here are some final steps you can take to start putting these ideas into practice:

1. **Start Small but Start Now**: Whether it's creating a budget, opening an investment account, or saving for a down payment on a home, the most important thing is to start now. Don't wait for the "perfect" moment or a higher salary. Even small steps today can lead to big results in the

future.
2. **Educate Yourself**: Financial literacy is a lifelong journey. Continue learning about personal finance, investing, and wealth-building strategies. Books, podcasts, and online courses can help you deepen your understanding and keep you on track.
3. **Build a Support System**: Surround yourself with people who share your goals and values. This could be friends, family members, or even online communities focused on financial empowerment. Having a support system can keep you motivated and accountable.
4. **Pass on What You've Learned**: One of the most powerful things you can do is share what you've learned with others. Talk to your children, your family, and your community about the importance of financial literacy and building wealth. By passing on this knowledge, you're helping to break the cycle of financial hardship for future generations.

A Final Word

This journey to financial freedom isn't easy, and it won't happen overnight. But every step you take is a step closer to breaking the chains of consumerism and building a future where financial stability and generational wealth are within reach.

It's important to remember that wealth isn't just about money—it's about freedom. The freedom to live life on your terms, the freedom to provide for your family, and the freedom to create opportunities for the next generation. That's the ultimate goal of everything we've discussed in this book.

CONCLUSION: RECLAIMING FINANCIAL POWER

So take the knowledge you've gained here, and use it to make a difference in your life. The road to financial freedom is long, but with the right mindset, the right tools, and the right actions, it's a journey you can absolutely complete.

Thank you for taking this journey with me. Now, let's get to work on creating the financial future you deserve.

Back Matter

Contact Information

For inquiries, feedback, or to connect with the author:
Dante Woodson
dantelwoodson@gmail.com

Privacy Policy

Your privacy is important to me. If you provide your email address or other personal information, it will be used solely for communication purposes related to this book. Your information will not be shared with third parties.

About the Author

Dante Woodson is an licensed real estate professional, entrepreneur and financial literacy advocate with a passion for helping individuals achieve financial freedom. He is dedicated to educating and inspiring others. Connect with him online for more resources and insights.

Terms of Use

Readers are granted a limited, non-exclusive license to use this book for personal, non-commercial purposes. Reproduction, distribution, or modification of any part of this book without permission is prohibited. This agreement may be terminated by either party if there is a breach of terms, with a written notice of 30 days required for resolution. This agreement shall be governed by the laws of the State of [Your State], without regard to its conflict of law principles.

Disclaimer

The information in this book is provided for educational and informational purposes only. It is not intended as legal, financial, or professional advice. The author and publisher are not responsible for any actions taken based on the information provided in this book.

Notes

Notes

Notes

www.ingramcontent.com/pod-product-compliance
Lightning Source LLC
Chambersburg PA
CBHW070356230526
45471CB00006B/2589